THE PATTERN OF POSSESSION

*The Purpose Driven Life They
Don't Want You To Know.*

JT Young

Order this book online at www.trafford.com
or email orders@trafford.com

Most Trafford titles are also available at major online book retailers.

Printed in Victoria, BC, Canada.

ISBN: 978-1-4269-3095-9 (sc)
ISBN: 978-1-4269-3096-6 (e-book)

Our mission is to efficiently provide the world's finest, most comprehensive book publishing service, enabling every author to experience success. To find out how to publish your book, your way, and have it available worldwide, visit us online at www.trafford.com

Trafford rev. 4/19/2010

 www.trafford.com

North America & international
toll-free: 1 888 232 4444 (USA & Canada)
phone: 250 383 6864 ♦ fax: 812 355 4082

Contents

This is just a bit of information for those of you that may wonder why I call the Lord,"Yeshua!"

I will be writing a book on this too but for now I will give you the short version as to why I know for a fact that the Lord's name is Yeshua and not Jesus because in this book I will be calling him ," Yeshua."

Fact 1.In the Websters Dictionary (Tenth Edition)Look up the name Jesus and you will see the Hebrew name of the Lord just before the definition." Yeshua."

Fact 2.In Matthew ch.1 : 21 Joseph,who is of Aramaic decent and speaks," Hebrew," is told by an angel what to name the Lord,The angel had to speak to Joseph in Hebrew,So he gave him the Hebrew name," Yeshua." Which is an original "Aramaic"name.

Fact 3.The definition for Jesus does not match the definition told to Joseph of what the holy child's name means,JESUS:for he shall save...wrong. Notice in the KJV the colon (:)after this is the definition.

Just like what is in most dictionaries,this is also in Matthew ch.1 verse 21.JESUS (:)for he shall save.

Fact 4.Yeshua in the Strong's Concordance in the very back in the Hebrew section #3442 show us that Yeshua or Yeshuwa : for he will save....word for word match with the definition gave by the angel to Joseph. This is the only name that means this.

Fact 5.If you go to China or anywhere and they ask you ,"What is your name?"You would just say your Name in English. No matter where you go your name is the same. Why is this different for Yeshua?

Fact 6.They must learn English to say your name right,you do not change your name every time you leave the U.S.,that is against the law and that is called an alias:an assumed or additional name.

Fact 7. Sense we know Mary and Joseph named our Lord the Hebrew name we should learn some Hebrew and say his name in Hebrew not English. Remember>>Acts 4 : 12,No other name.

Fact 8. If the Lord Yeshua was here in the holy land and got on a plane and flew to the U.S.A. and you Asked him,"Hey,what is your name?"He would not say Jesus,that would be lying,seeing that his passport would say his birth name from where he was born,which was in Nazareth,with the Jews and Aramaic people. In Nazareth they called him," Yeshua!"and also he cannot lie. Now I hope this Explains the name Because too many people get confused when trying to translate,spell,and transliterate the name of the Lord. None of this is needed because if you tried to spell the Lords name in another language it would turn out to be a different name than what he is " CALLED."This is why the bible says that whosoever shall ," CALL " upon the name of the Lord shall be saved.....Not whosoever translates...

We must simply call on his name,Yeshua,and it should remain the same no matter where he is preached.

There is so much scripture about the name of the Lord you would think we would know how Important it is to know his true name. Yeshua,Yeshuwa,As long as it sounds right...that is what matters. I hope this truly blesses you and I hope you use the revelation of information that is in this book and may the Lord bless you many times.

THE PATTERN OF POSSESSION

{The Purpose Driven Life they don't want you to know.}

First I would like to give honor to my heavenly Father and Yeshua Christ my lord in whom I have gave my life. I thank you for all you have done, are presently doing and will do in my life, I also would like to thank my wife for helping inspire me to write this book. I also would like to thank my pastor Daniel L. Turner and his wife Palestine Turner and the whole Gospel Mission Church family.

Now this book has information that all people need to know. This one little book will change the way you see and hear and reveal to you the nasty little secret about how your enemy is at work constantly right now in the lives,in the bodies of people. Now this information is quit simple to explain so it will not take much reading to comprehend where I am going so to make what you are about to read easy to remember and understand I will first tell you a story.......

Once upon a time there was a man who lived in Gadarenes which is over by Galilee

He was a certain man who lived all alone. One day as he was pulling up huge weeds out of his garden there came a man who offered to help him for free,however he needed a place to stay for he was wet and cold from the rain for it rained a lot there. So the certain man unwilling at first to let him stay finally agreed and let him in. Now he had some help and things went fine, he also had a good year in harvest and slowly became rich. Now his friend said ,"Now I will take my portion of the profits we made and leave!,"but secretly he was testing him to see what he would say.

So the certain man said ,"Please don't go, we are making so much money and I have yet to finish this brick wall we have begun to build, less I not have enough strength to finish it!"So at that saying the friend said," O.k. , O.k. keep your shirt on you old goat you."and he cursed a bit,just a little,this was to see if the certain man would permit it,for he has friends that act this way and he wanted to invite them to his house too. Now the certain man did not rebuke him nor question him about his attitude but now had doubts about whether he was his friend or not.

Just as the certain man began to think whether to even have him stay any longer there was a knock at the door...Now the house was a mess and the certain man wanted no company unless it was some one who knew his friend for he did not want to be bothered for he was counting money.

So his friend of a long time now answered the door and it was six of "his" friends who together makes seven. Now the certain man did not know that his friend went by night and told his six friends to come by, so the friend said unto the certain man,"Hey man pour us all some wine an lets celebrate for now we have plenty of help and no one can stop us now!"So the certain man at first was upset because his friend asked him to pour wine for he knew drinking wine was not wise,however they beckoned him and begged him so as children having no parents,so he swore a bit and cursed a bit,just a little....then he sat and drank with them. Now the house is in even a bigger mess and none of the seven would even swat a fly,for the men all drew flies. Worst still the land lord was to visit soon,but what could the certain man do? For there are seven of them and only one of him,so he in an uproar said as he cursed and drank yet more wine,"Hey, lets finish this brick wall you guys!"So they gave him strength and encouraged him and he felt strong and they helped him build the wall. Not only did they build a wall but many other things they did and profit was very good.

Now his friend had came up with a plan to expand their business, for profit was good with much fame and women and cattle and a wall around all their stuff. So there came a day when the friend told each of " his " friends to go and bring their friends too, for each one had six friends.

The friend of the certain man asked if this was O.K. ,But the man was busy chasing a woman and did not want to be bothered. Now if you can count you know that if each of the seven men went and got six more men that would look like this... 7 x 6 = 42 men.

Now there are forty-two men in the house and they all worked and drunk and were merry. So now profit is very good for they made much money and they became riotous and unruly even the certain man. For now after a long time they were good friends and they even bathed together, but not to be clean for they bathed in wine,and money and women. The land lord saw the prosperity of them and would have put them out but they bribed him with money. So they gave him much money and he for a while let them alone. Now the house is in even a bigger mess for all the men had no manners and did not listen to the certain man much,and a last,"what can I do,"said the certain man,for there was Forty and two of them and only one of him. Then there came a day when the land lord had enough of their foolishness because they ran around naked in the house , chased women , smelled bad and there was trash and clothes everywhere, for they never washed their cloths, therefore they had nothing to wear. Nor did they wash themselves so they bred more flies. There was a knock at the door,"It's the land lord,open this door now!"said the land lord. So they open the door and the certain man ripped the landlord's clothes off and one of the men killed him.

Now the neighbor of the certain man saw what he did and would have talked with him to help him even help him get rid of all these men but alas,"This big wall is in the way!"said the neighbor. and no one could speak to the certain man accept who his friends allowed.

So the neighbor sent a request to the king and the officers were sent and they bound the certain man and put him in prison. The friends of the certain man of a long time said",Let's all go and get more friends like us so that we may break these chains and fetters and be free!"

So each one went and got six more friends with himself made seven.

42 x 6 = 252

Great,"Now I will break these chains and fetters and go and hide in the cave."said the certain man. So he broke the chains and knock down the doors and fled. Now all the people gathered together to help the officers apprehend this fellow, because now he must be crazy or a lunatic by now, seeing how he breaks forth and runs and kills and no one man can tame. There came a day when the people came to help the certain man,(for they knew where he was.)and they would have helped him but,"Alas, this stupid wall is in the way!"they said. For he would not speak unto them or so much as even look at them,for this wall was around his mind..... and he thought only on what his friends said and cared not what the people said. So they caught him and bound him yet again and his friends said ,"We can help you but you must let us go and taketh more friends more wicked and stronger than ourselves!"So the certain man allowed them to do so for he was in a betwixt and knew not what to do. So each one went and got six more,more wicked than himself, and they came back and dwelt there.

252 x 6 = 1,512

Now the man had the strength of an ox, for his friends strengthened him like before, from within, for as you must know by now.....his friends are Demons.

So he broke the chains and killed much people and fled to a place he knew no one would come save they were dead...for he hated all people. So he went and dwelt among the tombs in the grave yard and no one would go near that place for fear of him and of Death who also became his friend. And his friend who was there at the beginning whose name was Greed said,

"We can rob and take from these graves!"and another of his friends said,"Let's cut ourselves!" for his name was Lunatic,and another of his friends said,"Let us kill anyone that comes by here!" on that saying they knew his name was Death. And of all that the Demons said unto him he would do, for there were 1,512 of them and only one of him.........

Now if I wanted to end this story on a good note I would say what is said in the bible in the book of Mark ch.5 vrs.1 through 20.BUT...sorry, this is usually how it ends,there is no happy ending without Yeshua Hamashiack,and it can only get worse from here as you can see the progression and the pattern.......this is how they work. It starts out small,only what you are willing to allow,but as the pattern takes effect,the wages of sin will be death.

I hope who ever reads this book understands that you must refer to the bible to see this clearly so get your bibles, you are about to see a Purpose Driven life they don't tell you about...what Satan does not want you know....I know this book will be a blessing to all that read it and I trust that you will refer back to it every time you are encountering a spiritual battle in your life,for the weapons of our warfare are not carnal but mighty through the

there, because nobody was home...and yet the body" is" home. This is the secret,"One will always go and get six!"666. Each one goes and gets six.666. Every time they leave they each come back with six.

This is their pattern, this is how they work in the lives of men,they don't play fair,and they stack the odds against you. And without devine help from God you can't win. It does not matter how much money you have or how many cars or houses you have," For a man's life does not consist in the abundance of things which he possess.... when he is possessed...see,(Luke ch.12 : 15)

You can also see the pattern starting in(Mark ch.8 : 36 - 37) with covetousness or "Greed" for short. There is nothing more important than your soul. No amount of things or money can buy it back once you loose it...Greed is the first demon that comes to visit you,And it is not always about money....So stop him at the door and say," I am content with the things I have and if I need anything my God will supply all of my needs according to his riches and glory in Christ Yeshua!" Bye..and slam the door, hang up the phone, turn the channel ,walk away,no Run...For he will come to you in many forms. So what I say unto you is ,"Watch... and pray."

See the Pattern

The Pattern in numbered form looks like this:

1 + 6 = 7 One goes and gets six,all together they are seven see-(Mark ch.16 : 9)

7 x 6 = 42 Each one goes and gets six.

42 x 6 = 252 Each one goes and gets six.

252 x 6 = 1,512 ....will be about 2,000 see- (Mark ch.5 : 13)

Now Greed is a serious problem, even to Kings. Look at the story of David and Bathsheba,see if you can see the start of the pattern of demon possession on his mind and when did he get delivered from these demons influence...(II Samuel ch.11 : 1 - 27 and ch.12 : 1 - 20)

Now if you have read the story you may have noticed some things that you were not aware of at first. David is walking on the roof of the house and he "sees" a woman washing herself.(2 Sam 11:2)You see how it starts,he could have just turned away quickly and said "Oops,I should not have seen that."But for some reason he kept looking....and looking...oooh..she looks good. still looking...?

This is the oldest trick in the book,if the demon can get you to look long enough,he can get inside of you and tell you to keep looking,you think it is you thinking to yourself,

"Man she is fine!" but your just repeating what that demon is saying as he speaks from within you.....but in order to really finish the job which is to steal,kill and destroy",this is their purpose," he will need some help.....

1 + 6 = 7 One goes and gets Six,this makes Seven.

(2Sam. 11:3-4)David "sent"messengers and inquired after the woman- you see it,right there..when he sent them,he sent for ,"THEM!!!",the help of the DEMONS. Normally a King of honor would never sleep with another man's wife,especially the wife of a soldier of his army,so when someone does something out of their character.....someone else is driving the controls leading and guiding them,"a demon."However a covetous or greed demon for short ,only knows how to be covetous or greedy, that's it. Now he must get David to steal or take her,but only if that is what David wants. Because demons are spirits,and at this early stage in the pattern, they can't make him do anything. So Greed goes and gets Theft,the result is...(verse 4.)Also in this same verse David lay with her, (sex)which was caused by (Adultery). (2Sam. 11 : 6 - 8)

Now David sends for Uriah after finding out that Bathsheba is pregnant. He needs to know weather Uriah knows about it or not so he will start some meaningless conversation about anything just to see what Uriah would say."So Uriah, uum,hows things goin with Joab?"Notice ,he could have confessed all he did,but obviously (Deceit),"another demon,"was there running his mouth. So David told Uriah to go to his house and he bribed him with a mess of meat.

(verse 9 - 12)

Uriah did not go to his house as you can see, so he did not fall for that trick altogether. Of corse this made David upset and he needed more help because now he needs to get rid of Uriah before he finds out about his wife.

(7 x 6 = 42) seven goes and gets six...this makes 42

Now David needed time to devise a plan,(verses 13 - 15,) so he tells Uriah to stay until tomorrow. David then feeds him to the full and gets him drunk..(Gluttony)and Uriah laid on his kings bed with the servants of his lord the king...(Adultery)(Fornication) and (Orgy)or Legion,"When many people get together for sexual indulgence," of corse while this is going on the demons are there too, so it is " Legion,"or many. Remember all of this is done is secret because this whole book is a secret....this is the Purpose Driven life they don't want you to know. This is what happens," behind reality,"in spirituality. Notice verse 14 - 15,he writes a letter to Joab,and sent it by ,"Uriah!"Now how slick and subtle is that. Uriah brings his own death sentence,and doesn't even know it.

Because it is a secret....The letter says to put Uriah in front of the hottest battle that he may die!(Death)and this is the sixth one. So know their names,1 Deceit ,2 Gluttony, 3 Adultery, 4 Fornication, 5 Legion, 6 Death. I use the weapons of influence that the demons use on people to name them,because you are what you do.....not who you say you are.

None of this would have happened if David would have said "NO!" when Greed told him to keep looking. That demon always running his mouth....he needs to shut up.

If he would have known that's who was at the door of his heart knocking trying to get in, he would not have even gave him the time of day, and this story would have had a different ending. So when you know how it starts,you can stop it before it gets out of control. So know who is doing the talking and who is driving....and if you find yourself or someone else doing something they normally would never do....it could be a demon trying to get in...It's a good thing David knew how to repent and pray for forgiveness. Remember, no matter how many times you fall, you must get back up. Now I know you may wonder,"how can someone who is saved and serving the Lord fall so easy or commit a sin to start with?"When you have the Holy Spirit how can you still sin against God. Whether on purpose or by accident we all will sin at some point. Sometimes we will commit a sin and not even know it. This is why it is good to pray all the time. However if you know the pattern of the temple, how we are set up and made in the spirit, then you will be able to see how it is possible for even the most holy of people to slip up like David did.

We are the temple......

>>>>>>> (1 Corinthians ch.3 : 16 - 17) <<<<<<<<<<<<

THE TEMPLE

If you read this then you know I am not making this up......we are temples now,just like in the old testament and the Spirit of God is in us. Now here is were the problem comes in at.......To many people do not know exactly how the temple was built and set up. So Knowing the pattern of the temple means knowing about yourself. The temple was made in the,"Patterns of things in the Heavens."(Hebrews 9 : 23)In other words it is the physical pattern of your spiritual self. The temple pattern has three parts.

The Temple: Utter Court Inner Court Holiest of All " 3 "

Our body : Body = Flesh ----Soul = Feelings ---Spirit = Life " 6 "

3 + 6 = 9 Nine fruits of the spirit. We must possess these 9 fruits.

The Utter Court is our body which is our flesh,this is why I put it under the words" Utter Court."

The Inner Court has our soul and feelings,this is why these words are under "Inner Court."

line of defense and with the life that most people live It is easy for a demon to get in. We must protect the Utter Court,by doing so we can stop a lot of problems before they even start.

>> Inner Court (Ezekiel ch.44 : 15 - 17 and 21) <<

Only the priests were allowed into the inner court and they had to wear certain cloths. They could not just go before God looking any kind of way,this is in verse 17.Remember they went to the utter court to the people,this is in verse 19.They also could not drink wine or beer or any alcohol when they entered into the inner court. This is in verse 21.This court is a place for worship.

INNER COURT

Worship deals with your feelings. So do not let any one fool you and say, " It don't matter how you feel."

We are not robots and we cannot just do something anyway even though we feel bad about it. We were made this way for a reason, So that we can worship, "I AM,"(Exodus 3:14) and also (John 8:58) the living God who's name is "Ehyeh in Hebrew. Now here is the big secret about worship...what makes you feel good? What makes you happy ? What excites you?How do you have fun?Our God wants us to go to him for happiness,joy,love and all those things that makes us feel good, you know those "fruits of the spirit."(Galatians ch.5 : 22 - 23)

These are feelings by the way.

(John ch.16 : 24)He wants us to ask the Father" Ehyeh," in his name...." Yeshua!",be patient and wait on him.....

So that our joy may be full. This is true worship,when you" feel " the love of Ehyeh and you cry out for more. When you show love,joy,peace,patience,gentleness,goodness,faith,meekness and temperance.

But many times we make the mistake of using a substitute in order to get our joy and happiness. Remember the Holy Spirit is a comforter. >>> (John 16 : 7) <<< So do you feel comfort in your life or do you feel like you need a drink......and I'm not talking about water or kool-aid. Are you relaxed or do feel like you need a smoke........humm ?

All the wrong things that people allow in their body is the result of trying to fill the emotional needs of ," Worship." Wait, it gets worse...just who do you think provides all these other ways of feeling good. The very one who wants your worship instead of giving it to Ehyeh the living God,

" Satan!"

(Matt.ch.4 : 8 - 9) Remember Satan wants you to worship him. Remember it matters how you feel,this is how we are to seek the Lord....with our feelings.

>> (Acts ch.17 : 27) Seek first the Kingdom of God with your feelings. Remember this...you must guard your heart.(Prov. 4 : 23) for out of it flows the issues of life. This is what it is all about..... Control of your emotions. In the Inner Court you poured out your heart to the Lord,you didn't hold back,you didn't care who was looking,you cried out for help. Why do people argue? Emotions. Why do people fall in love?

Emotions. Just about every aspect of your life and mine is controlled by emotions,or feelings. If you feel like it you will do it,and if you do not feel like it you will not.....Right. Now why do you think an emotion is called an " Emotion,"well because E = m. Here I go getting all scientific again.

If energy makes mass then energy makes motion. Energy=Motion....

E motion....get it?

You see,in the Inner Court you can be controlled and made to do things and of course commit sin. This is known by demons and this is why almost all activity you are exposed to is purposely made to make you feel a certain way. However this is a form of control that needs an immediate reaction from you or else it will not work. This is why it is good to think about what you are going to do before you do it. You know,count to ten or something. This is why we so much need to develop the fruit of the spirit called ,"Temperance."The Christian that is mature in this area of the spirit is usually a calm,well mannered person who is not defeated by this tactic and can successfully guard his gate to his Inner Court.

Committing a sin is one thing,but doing it and "feeling ,"like it is o.k. Is another. When that happens,no one even asks for forgiveness,and this is the true intent of the demon,to get you to "feel" like it's o.k.."Now," you are sinning on purpose,and that is direct disobedience, and the Wrath of God commeth on the children of disobedience .

>>>>>>>>>>> Holiest of All <<<<<<<<<<<<

In the book of Hebrews chapter 9 starting at verse 2 it shows you what was in this part of the temple.

Also you find out that only the high priest went in alone once every year. (Now Yeshua is our high priest).In this part of the temple there was the golden censer,and the ," Ark Of The Covenant."In the ark was a golden pot that had manna, Aaron's rod that budded, and the tables of the covenant,"The Ten Commandments."Now you see what should be in your holiest of all, (spirit).The manna shows provision of sustenance...what sustains you or keeps you alive. The rod is budding because there is life growing in it and the rod shows correction,if you spare the rod you spoil the child. Also the Ten Commandments of God that if we obey them we will live a perfect life before him. This is the most important place in you.....where your spirit is. Now the Lord Yeshua the anointed one is the true bread from heaven,he is the manna now,the Holy Spirit is correcting and guiding you and the ten commandments are to be inside of you.>>>> Hebrews ch.8 : 10 <<<< Now this is in our minds and hearts,not on stone tables. This is the place that is under attack by the enemy,this is his whole purpose for possessing you to start with,so that he can get in your " holiest of all " and be the one who teaches you and lead you and guide you ....to hell. However we are suppose to let the Lord Yeshua into our heart....not devils.

Remember we are all temples now. So Guard your gates ye yoke fellows.

Obey the Commandments,Produce those fruits,and have faith in the Lord. Those are the main things you ,me and anyone should be focusing on...those three things.

1. The Ten Commandments

2. The Fruits of the Spirit

3. Faith in Yeshua the Lord.

And for those of you who are trying to be grace riders and say that we do not need to worry about the law,(Ten Commandments)this is what the Lord says,

>>>> Matthew 5 : 17 – 20 <<<<<<

You must do and teach these Ten Commandments. If you continue to read pass verse 20 you will see that he is truly talking about those same ten commandments that was gave to Moses on mount Sinai. So many of us do not get much teaching on those ten commandments and many people are breaking them and do not know it. An example of this is the now obvious fact that thousands of people go to the synagogue or church on Sunday. Our Lord Yeshua had a good habit of going to the church on the Sabbath day,not on Sunday,in fact the bible says it was his custom to do so,>>>(Luke 4 : 16)Now I am not speaking against church on Sunday, But what are you doing on the Sabbath day. Hummm? Thou shalt remember the sabbath day and keep it holy. Now if you are thinking,"Hey,that was for our forefathers."Well read this>>>

(Jer. ch.17 : 21 – 22)

Even though this generation of people was not even there when they came out of Egypt,they still had to keep the sabbath day."as I commanded your fathers."

Your Holy of Hollies is under attack.......So fight the good fight of faith.

How can you win the good fight of faith if you don't know who your fighting against. We all have an adversary,someone who is against us,who hates us,and if they could they would kill us... never forget this,because they will not. First of all people are not your enemy. Your boss,your neighbor, that person that is always getting on your nerves. No,I will show you who they are.

Know Your Enemy

(Mark ch.7 : 20 - 23)

Evil thoughts, Adultery ,Fornication, Murder, Theft, Covetousness, Wickedness, Deceit, Lasciviousness, Evil eye, Blasphemy, Pride, Foolishness, All these evil things are demons... spirits working in the bodies of people,but only if we let them in. Look at verse : 19 They enter into the heart,(the Soul and Mind)and they defile from inside. Remember the first one"Evil thoughts!"

(1 Timothy ch.6 : 10 - 12)

In order to fight our enemy we must cut him off at the root! this is the only way to get rid of them. Notice that before we are told to fight the good fight of faith we are told the root cause of all evil. Here he is again,running his mouth, "Covetousness" but I call him,"Greed!!"see-(verse 10).Now remember the words that are used and see if this makes sense to you. The tree and it's fruit you can see,but the roots of that tree you can't see."Because they are deep underground, inside the earth." You can't see them, but that does not mean they are not there....

You are the earth....the roots are spirits....

When you are pierced through with sorrows these are unclean spirits that are mind piercing,like a crown of thorns they stab into the mind of the unknowing victim. Now lets backtrack the scripture and find the weapon to fight this spirit with.........(1 Timothy.ch6 : 6 - 8) Godliness with "contentment".Being content with what you already have can stop Greed at the door and he will never get in you,or me, or anybody.

David already had three wives (1 Sam. 25 : 42 - 44).We must realize that there is always someone more less fortunate than us,just when we think we got it bad....someone else got it worse!

If you are living paycheck to paycheck, someone is not getting a check. You may feel sick,but someone is dying of something. You may have went through a divorce,but someone has never had the pleasure of being with anyone. So be content with what you already have and if you need help,God will help you,"He helped me!" Because godliness with contentment is great gain....

Now that you know how to fight Greed,lets read about some more of your enemies that you need to be warned about.....

Know Your Enemy

Adultery and Fornication. These two demons are good friends. One of them tries to get people who are married to have sex with someone else other that their spouse that they already have. The other tries to get people to have sex without even getting married.

It starts like this (Matthew ch.5 : 27 - 29) When a man or woman looks at someone else,and just "wants to have sex,"with them, they have just that quick, let(Adultery) in there mind through the eye gate. Remember the heart is the mind. Now that Adultery is in there he will need some help to get them to do what he is telling them. This is where(Fornication)steps in....

Now Fornication says," Just do it man!"Then (Theft)helps tricks them into stealing this person from their spouse....

{ If it sounds like you read this already that's because you are seeing the pattern...}

Now (Deceit)comes along and helps them cover it up so that no one will know about it. This way by the time anyone can render a reason,"Oops, it's to late!" And to make a long story short,(Death) finally shows up when a Jealous husband finds out and kills them...Because however you lay down and die that is how you will get up. You see the secret Purpose that is Driving these demons is they want you dead and they want you to feel guilty and lost and die that way.

You see if you die this way, they know that once your in Hell there is no escape,and they can torment you and beat you and rip off your flesh and stab your heart and laugh while you cry...... Because they work for Satan,and Satan hates you....yes SATAN,you know him? THE DEVIL....whell he knows you.

(1 Peter ch.5 : 8) He is your adversary looking around to see if he can get you caught up in the pattern! This is his engine of sin and all he need you to do is start it,"Just turn the key!"COMON,"JUST DO IT!!"

Once the engine is started,he steps back and let it run, it will run until it runs out of gas,then it dies....

So remember if you don't start it,you will not die in the car of sin,"Don't even get in it!"I know it looks nice,with them 24 inch rims with a rubber ban for a tire,(low profile tires.)and that candy pretty paint job. Dont forget the boom,with the amps and subwoofers all in da trunk.....and that loud mouth, tricked out exhaust.. OOOhhh,look it even has all white leather inside,smells new,and it even has a flip down navigation screen and CD player.... And look at the T.V. screens in the front and the back..Boy these seats are soft and they are heated..

HOOOOLD UP!!!," WAIT A MINUTE!!!!" WHY ARE YOU READING THIS PART,

I TOLD YOU NOT TO GET IN THE CAR,YOU SITTIN ALL ON THE,.. MAN, TURN THE PAGE!!!

Anyway you see how easy it is to get caught up in the" car of sin."Don't you already have a car?Do you really need another one. Just kidding.... I don't care how many cars you get,don't get that one.

THE DEVIL AND HIS ANGELS.

Do you know that the devil has angels too? (Revelation ch.12 : 9 - 10)Not only was the devil cast out of heaven down to earth but also his angels are cast out with him. Notice what the devil was doing in verse 10,Running his mouth.

That is all he does,that slick talkin Devil. He constantly tries to convince God that you are not good enough to live in heaven on earth, and to have eternal life. He always points out your shortcomings,"See, look at them!"he says. He wants you to loose your faith in God,pointing to you,accusing you...."They all have sinned,and come short remember!"he says."You here that,he just lied,and he's jay walking!"he says. He is like a corrupt lawyer showing evidence on you,"Look we got him on video!"he says. Just read what he said standing before God concerning Job,(Job ch.1 :6-12)

Even then Satan had his angels helping him destroy all that Job had. Because Satan can not be everywhere at once,and all that happened to Job happened so fast that before one person could finish a sentence there came another person with bad news then another.....while he was yet speaking,another and while he was yet speaking,another and while he was yet speaking,another ...(Job ch.1 : 14 - 19)

Remember Satan has to go to and fro and walk up and down in the earth,he cannot be everywhere at once,he is not omni- present everywhere,he is bound by this rule.(Job ch.1 : 7) not by real chains. He is a spirit and you cannot bind a spirit with chains.

Many people think that the angels that were cast out of heaven are bound in chains in hell,(2 Peter ch.2 : 4)but remember,the bible is a spirit book,only one who has the Holy Spirit of God can understand it.....Can you hold a spirit in a chain,how about an invisible angel that has the strength of a thousand men. I remember a story about a certain man who could not be held with chains....he broke them! and you think an angel (2 Peter 2 : 11) that is greater in power and might can be held with chains?.......

You may say,"But they are chains of darkness!"Can the darkness hold anything,come on!

They are simply "Reserved" or Saved for the day of judgment. This means God has not cast them in the lake of fire yet. This is where the whole chain thing comes from...(Revelation ch.20 : 1 -3)Remember this has not happened yet.

Just like all the people that are willfully sinning are not in hell yet....There are still killers out there,liars,thieves, and if you are not aware of this, they will catch you unaware and steal from you or worse, kill you because your guard was down. You thought they were in jail. They laugh because you think they are not there...... but they are. These are the demons,the devils...the bad angels. Remember

(Mark ch.5 : verse 12).All demons are also called devils and Satan is also called the devil and he is a fallen angel, so all devils are like ," The Devil !"They are fallen from grace and they know it. The Devil And His Angels

Now if you refer back to (Revelation ch.12 : 9 - 13)you see that the devil, "Satan" and his angels are cast to the earth. Verse 12. shows you that he "and his angels,"are down her among us and they are mad.He is very upset at God and persecutes the saints,the church and anyone he can find fault with. Notice in verse 13.He persecutes like a prosecuting attorney,judging you before God... and to persecute simply means to:

Persecute - to pursue or harass in a manner designed to injure,grieve or afflict. To cause to suffer because of belief. To annoy with persistent or urgent approaches,

In other words,"To get on your nerves,to bother you all the time,to discourage you and tell you, "you can't do that!"To run their mouth and persuade you to think less of yourself,To tell you,"You can't believe in God," To tell you your not ready to get saved...."you are really not saved."To persuade you,trick you. They can not kill you or make you do anything,but they are subtle,and this is what makes them dangerous,they are so slick, they talk people into doing stupid stuff like:

smoking , drinking alcohol , lying , stealing , cheating , killing and all that stuff,they can't make a nat move but they can lie to a camel and he will do just what they say. They influence some to kill themselves. They whisper negative things into your spirit."You can't lose weight!" or "You can't make enough money!"

Notice while Satan and his angels are down here it does not say that the angels are bound. No, they continue to run around putting negative thoughts in the minds of men, running their mouth,they need to"Shut up!" Remember the everlasting Lake of Fire was prepared for the Devil,"And His Angels!"

(Matthew ch.25 :41)
Notice... " They have not been cast in the Lake of Fire yet !!!!!!"

So if anyone tries to tell you,"Oh don't worry about those evil angels,they are bound up in chains,"just tell them to read this book or better yet have them to read (Revelation ch.12 : 9 - 13).It

29

does not say anywhere that they are bound,"yet." The good book says we perish because we don't know......they don't want you to know. They would rather you believe they are bound, so that they can bind you........

This is their camouflage,and this is what they hide behind..... your unbelief,your ignorance....

How can you see what you don't believe is there......But I hope that reading this book snaps us all back to reality, like on the movie " Men In Black 2 " when " K " slowly started getting his memory back. He began to see things that were already there,things that 90% of people do not see,and if they try to tell someone about it, they are called crazy or something.

Yes the Devil and " his " angels are here, now,Can you see them.....

The Devil and His Angels.

Have you ever noticed that some people say they have a problem with something but don't know why?

Or someone may say,"I don't know why this keeps happening to me."They know what is happening,they just don't know why...... or who. It is who's causing the problem....not why. So many people fall for this one little trick. It's kinda like playing pool if you have ever played this game. Remember,it's not about the fact that you keep getting hit in the back of the head,you just need to turn to the person who is doing the hitting and tell them to stop,in the name of Yeshua. Satan thinks your not worthy of the blessings of God. Do you know what he thinks about you?

(Job 4 : 12 - 19)

One of Job's friends chooses to put his two cents in this situation that Job is in. Eliphaz says some things that sounds like he thinks Job is going through this because he has done something wrong and he is reaping what he sowed. Then he says he has a ,"Secret",that was told to him in a dream by a spirit....hummm.

Now remember that Satan has been messing with Job all through this book,now he turns one of his friends against him and if you really study what Eliphaz says this spirit said....then you know it is not God talking to him....it is Satan. Now really break down the 18th and 19th verse and you will see that Satan thinks that God can not trust you because God cast him and the angels that were with him out of heaven. So if God can not trust Satan,who is an angel,how can he trust you?You see we are them that dwell in houses of clay.

So let us prove him wrong and show the world that we can be trusted because we trust in Yeshua the True Messiah and he has redeemed us from the world. We can live a holy life in Christ and enter into the kingdom of God as long as we don't let Satan talk us out of it. Remember that those angels that follow Satan had been in the kingdom but left their own habitation (Jude verse 6)and they fell from heaven to the depths of the earth as the Lord said (Luke ch.10 : 18)Satan fell like lightning....the negative electric energy of the world.

And he continues to feed off of all the negative energy with his angels. Look at how he fed off of Eilphaz in the book of Job 4 : 15.Notice how the hair of Eliphaz skin stood up........Static electricity. This is Negative energy from Eliphaz to Satan caused by Eliphaz's negative thinking about Job. He thought Job had sinned and did wrong and that he was receiving payback for the wrong he had done. Instead he should have been speaking good things to Job and encouraging him,saying positive things. The Devil and his angels are the one's behind the scene doing the feeding with you in the book of Jude.

They also use any type of trick to cause fear and negativity and then feed off of it....Like scary movies.

Think about it,a theater full of people all sending out emotional negative energy....that is a lot of energy and guess who wants it...... Jude 6 starts it of with the bad angels then verse 9 talks of more angelic stuff then you get to verse 12, ahhh... now you see what is really going on.....they feast with," you, '' feeding themselves. Now certain traits of angels are exposed in these two verses. They are like clouds carried by the wind. And who is the prince and power of the wind.....Satan >>(Ephesians 2 : 2).They are like raging waves,which are moved by the wind. And what was it that attacked Yeshua(Jesus) and his disciples as they went to the other side...........?

(Mark ch.4 : 35 - 39) Wind and Waves. Now this is why the wind and waves obeyed him,he was not talking to the storm,he was talking to those bad angels that was causing the storm. He was not crying about being hit in the head,he spoke to the one doing the hitting and told them to stop. In these same verses in Jude you see they are like wandering stars....And who are the seven stars of the seven churches ?(Rev. 1 : 20)The stars are angels, so the book of Jude is not just talking about ungodly men but also about the one's that cause men to be ungodly......Fallen Angels and Satan.

"Shhh, They Have A Purpose, And They Are Driven......."

So now you know the pattern,you have seen the pattern,you know your enemy,but can you see your enemy?Remember,you can't fight what you can't see....but even a blind man knows what his enemy sounds like..So don't always go by what things look like,for the Devil is changed into an angel of light.(2 Corinthians ch.11 : 14) He does not have red horns,he does not look like Hell boy..He is a disobedient angel and he has a purpose,an agenda.

(Isaiah ch.14 : 12 - 14)

Satan has a lot of nerve,maybe because he knows he is an eternal being that can't die...an Angel. and he wants to be over everything. He wants his own throne,and he wants it to be above God."What a fool."He wants to be worshiped and have total control of the church and the world..."He wants to be like the most high!"but higher.....And many people are going to be disappointed when they see what he really looks like."A Prosecuting Attorney."Just a bigmouth angel,always running his mouth.(verse 16)They will say," Is this it?"I though you was a big dragon or lion or,"wait ,the bible did say you were "AS "a roaring lion,not that you are ,or is or.....well..anyway.

This is his Purpose,to be the boss...And he has help. He is the one making accusations against you, me,everyone. And " HIS "Angels are helping him to do what he wants done. He will use any type of tactic to seduce,trick or fool even the very elect if it was possible....but there is information out there like this book,and if enough people are aware of his plans and his purpose, it will be that much harder for him to win....so let's fight the good fight of faith...

So why does he hate you so much?He hates me too!Everyone as far as he is concerned can live in Hell.

He hates us with a passion. This is part of the driving force that pushes at him constantly,every time he see's one of us. Why,simple.....just read this>>>(Genesis ch.1 : 26) Not only did God kick Satan out of Heaven...God makes us...And we look just like God, you know, "I AM THAT I AM",(Ehyeh Asher Ehyeh) the one who kicked out Satan. Not only that, but then God gives us dominion over all the earth. To rule over it all. The birds,cows,ducks,fish,...Everything,and what ever we name it,that is what it is called. Wow,so basically we are in control....This is what Satan wanted...I can just imagine Satan having a fit,"How dare he give the earth to them!",They are not worthy of it!"This is his purpose,and he will argue his case against you. He will run his mouth and blaspheme and lie.He is the father of lies. He has fooled those people who worship him and his angels and are just using them to help fulfill his will. Notice in Isaiah 14 verse 12. if you use a reference of the name Lucifer you will find that it also means Day Star. In most dictionaries this name means morning star.

"Shhh, They Have A Purpose,
And They Are Driven......"

Just look at what happened in the book of Jude.(Jude verse 9)Notice they are not throwing punches. They are Disputing about the body of Moses. This is how you will contend with the Devil,so study your Bibles and get your facts strait....this is how you will fight the good fight of faith. By protecting your faith,your confidence in God. Protect your belief in God...Fight to keep your mind on God's word. Fast and pray to build up your faith. Get ready for the dispute,the debate in the spirit. Know the truth.

Dispute- To engage in argument, to argue irritably or with irritating persistence,to struggle against,oppose.

Contend- To strive or vie in contest or rivalry or against difficulties.

Like I said before....Satan needs to," Shut up... " If he could, he would cause you to think your name is not really what you say it is. Is it?,"No it is not..", Yes it is." No it is NOT!" ... " YES IT IS!!"

You must hold on to the truth with a fighting persistence and you can not take down,not even for a second. Tell the truth , shame the devil ,Don't try to climb the mountain,tell it to move out of your way !!!

According to (Deuteronomy ch.34 : 5 - 6)The Lord buried Moses in a place that no man knows....but,

Satan chooses to fuss about Moses body...He hates Moses and anyone who knows him. Get thee behind me Satan!The Lord is still rebuking him even now...every time he see you or me. Yes I know I have wrote about things that are hidden,secrets of the enemy..But wait, I will tell you more secrets.....If you've ever heard about negative thoughts,Negative energy,a negative attitude...The dark side of the Universe,anything bad....... It's Demons..Fallen Angels, period.

What a checkered web they have made,to fool the world. Follow the checkered floor.

And yes, that is the physical pattern that they use to represent themselves traveling and communicating in and out of this world.

From the dark side to the light side and back again. From the spirit world into our world,into us. Just start opening your eyes to this fact and you will see the pattern of possession everywhere. Like in most movies.

Have you noticed that in just about every major motion movie picture there is that same pattern?The Matrix,Max Payne,even in that movie

"Precious,"in the classroom....the floor. Just look around and you will see the pattern. It is everywhere.....Right in front of you this whole time and you probably did not notice this until you read this book. You see the Devil is slick and cunning,and he has help. He has fallen angles helping him and he wants your worship. This is what that seen in Max Payne was all about,when he was on the floor on his, "Knees"and the ceiling burned away and the fallen angel came and stood before him. Hummm?

All you gotta do is open your eyes....you will see the truth.
The Pattern Of Possession is everywhere!!!

THEY WORK IN SECRET!

Remember the story about David? (2 Samuel ch.11 : 1 - 27) and (ch.12 : 1 - 12)Look at verse 12 in the 12th chapter of 2 Samuel....Notice how he did it secretly?...This is how they work," in secret!"

(Matthew ch.13 : 24 - 28) and (verse 37 - 39)

Notice that while men slept,the enemy came and sowed tares.. bad seed. The enemy that sowed them is the Devil. In the dark... at night....Most crimes happen at night. If the devil is so big and bad then why does he come while they are sleep. Look at (John ch.3 :19 - 20) some people love darkness because no one can see what they are doing. They must have something to hide,in the dark. Hiding things is a sure sign of demonic influence that leads up to possession and ," The Pattern."

Many people have secrets in their heart,(emotions) and they think no one will know but when you are in the midst of Holy Ghost filled Christians that know who their enemy is...they know and see the secrets and call them out.(1 Corinthians 14 : 24 - 25)Yes there are secrets in the hearts of men. But,(Romans ch.2 :16)

Say's there is coming a day when God will judge the " Secrets," of men.........

When you confess your secrets to God,they are no longer secrets,and there will be no secrets to judge against you. This is how you judge and examine yourself,and one of many reasons why prayer is important.

Have you ever notice how sometimes people " Whisper "...Why are you whispering?This is a sign,someone is talking in secrete.(Proverbs ch. 16 : 27 - 30)All of these verses go together because they all point to the lips...your mouth,and what you do with it. notice that a whisperer breaks up friendships...this is evil...it is demonic. The bad angels are influencing people to say the wrong things.

Think about it,why should you have to whisper,unless you don't want anyone to know what you are saying...Maybe you are at a funeral or there is prayer going on...still...why are you even talking while prayer is going on. So unless you have a sore throat,do not whisper unless you really must do so.

Let all things be done decently and in order..... it is out of order to whisper during prayer,preaching,even at a funeral. An it is a dead giveaway. That is how demons work," in secret..."

Let your yea be yea and your nay be nay....anything more than that brings evil,"demons."Whispering is just a tool that demons use to get inside your mind.(John ch.18 : 20)Yeshua never said nothing in secret unless it was a parable,So look out for (Whisperers).

This is why Christians must live a transparent lifestyle...we do not need secrets.

(Alcohol)another demon that goes unknown for a long time but now I will expose him...

It's easy to tell when someone is possessed by" this "one,they drink alcohol and they think it is o.k. to do so,and will fight for this right. But did you know that when someone drinks alcohol,

"They are drinking a spirit!"No,really!!! It even says it on most bottles...."Spirits!" Is this a co-incidence, are is there a reason why alcohol or wine is also called....."Spirits" hummm?

Just walk into a winery and say," Hey where da spirits at!!" They will tell you to look around man...(Joel ch.2 : 28-29)Yes spirits can take liquid form and be poured out. I know this sounds strange at first...but when you understand the laws of physics you know that nothing goes away,it simply changes form....think about water for instance. Water can evaporate...but it is not gone,it is just "Vapor"....It can condense in the air and form "Clouds ".... then when the density is right in the cloud walla,It comes back as"Rain,"because it never went anywhere. It just changed form. Spirits do this all the time,how do you think they get in us... Through sound waves,as vibrations....Foods digested...invisible Vapors inhaled....as Smoke, and yes" Liquids" that are drunk. This is what the picture on the cover of this book is all about. They are everywhere, everywhere. Remember,the spirit world was here first....make no mistake about this,and everything we see and are, came after it....God,the Angels,Satan and Heaven,was all here before us.....

Make no mistake,the spirit realm is the real world....we came from it.

Think about this,I have a younger brother that use to drink a long time ago. We were riding in his car one day and he had been drinking. So he says,"Hey,I gotta take a leak!"so I assumed that we were going somewhere so that he could use the bathroom.....but he did something no normal person in there right mind would do.... He stopped on the side of the road and got out of the car,"while traffic passed by and people walked by,"and he took a leak. That's when I knew he was not my brother...he was someone else. He even talked different,with a slur.

Stranger still he did not remember everything that happened that night. Of course he woke up with a hangover,but what do you expect to feel like,when a demon takes over your body then leaves it in a mess...

When people get drunk they do things they normally would not do. This is because they are being controlled by someone else...a DEMON!! This demon has a specific assignment,to posses and control people with alcohol. The alcohol is simply just the tool he uses to get inside you. Through your mouth gate, " remember the temple."

Another demon that needs to be exposed is (Pornography) Or ,"Lust" for short.

This is a wicked one. He simply uses familiar forms like,Maga zines,Movies,DVD's,Adult websites,any type of seeing format to posses you. He enters in through the eye gate and stains an image on the brain. He then uses your ability to imagine things,and he uses this against you by going to get (Adultery).Remember(Matthew ch.5 : 28)Notice how "Lust" comes first then"Adultery."It all started with a look....then a double take...well you get the picture. Some may think this is going to far but wait, there is more! Porn,Greed and Satan are attempting to take over the world and bring our morals down to nothing. Most commercials on T.V are sexually oriented in some slick way....sex this, sexy that.....It's bad when a broom sings to a woman,"baby come back!" Here's how he will do it. First with magazines, pictures,commercials and movies then the big finish....." The Internet!"The best way to fight this demon of porn for any man that may be having this problem is quite simple...Just enjoy your life with the wife of thy youth.... Not married,then get married.

If you know anything about the internet what you are about to read may be unbelievable......but believe it anyway. Read this...(Zechariah ch.5 : 1 - 11)If you read this you see a flying roll ,"that is a satellite!"

Yes that is what it is ....It is a curse that goeth forth over the face of the whole earth!(v.3)

It will be in everyone's house,(v.4)There is a woman inside of it(v.7)This is wickedness and it has a lead top like a satellite(v.8) Two women come out of it,and it is between the heaven and the earth.(v.9)And it has a,get ready for this," A Satellite Base !"(v.11)....Wow..Television and The Internet is in every ones house.....

Hummmmm......Do you remember how that stars are angels.... (Rev. ch.1 : 20) and how that Satan,also called Lucifer is a bad angel. Remember (Isaiah ch.14 : 12 - 14) Lucifer is also called Day Star. And where have you heard that name before.... hummmm?Now if you look at(Acts ch.7 : 43) you see the meaning of this star stuff..." The star of their god,"...Remphan a.k.a.

Baal a.k.a. Lucifer a.k.a. Baphomet a.k.a. Santa a.k.a. Satan... etc. All these names are to fool hide and confuse......the main point here is our God is not a star....The Devil is. And our Lord's name is not this Jesus that they keep pushing on all of us....His name is Yeshua.(Strong's #3442)and Matt. 1:21.Just look it up for yourself.

People are not going to come out publicly and say they worship Satan,It is a Secret.............

Most people do not even know they are being used by Satan. This is because he is a deceiver and his weapon of choice is...." Influence!" It has always been about influence.

Just watch the movie

" Training Day "and notice how the bad cop gets the new rookie to do bad things." INFLUENCE!!"

THE BATTLE FIELD!...

What about (Smoking).This one is simple. When a temple fills up full of smoke,if you are inside and you can't see or breathe... what will you do." Now when I asks people this question,they hesitate."You will get out ,right!Uuuum yea.. So if you are the temple of the Holy Ghost...and you start smoking,the Holy Ghost Leaves.....He cannot stay Inside you if you willingly put him out and chooses (Nicotine) instead. Once you allow Nicotine in, he then goes and get's (Monoxide) and (Poison)and(Addiction) and(Asthma) and(Cancer)and also(Death.)6 of them.

This is the pattern...this is how they work...It all starts in the Mind,with one...Greed!

What a lot of prosperity get rich preachers forgot to tell people is that you have an enemy constantly trying to stop you all the time. I tell you the spiritual side of the matter because thoughts are spiritual not physical. There lies the problem....Your" Mind" is operated by spirit, thus your mind and body is ," The Battle Field!" Without your spirit, your mind is just a hunk of flesh...useless.

The spiritual can become physical. Angels did it all through the bible. They are spirit beings but they roll away stones(Matthew ch.28 : 2)and in (Genesis ch.32 : 24 - 30) and (Hosea ch.12 : 2 - 4) Jacob wrestles with an Angel. So

S = E = MC2

All energy comes from the spirit world. If.......thought's are spiritual,and spiritual can become physical....

Then ," Thoughts can become Physical! "and manifest in this world.

They fire off neurons in the brain,that is energy...in your mind.

This is why your mind is the battle field,this is where you fight the good fight of faith. No it will not be easy,but it is yet so simple. The fight is within you,all the time. Positive and Negative,Good and Bad,God and Satan..... God wants you to have eternal life,Satan wants you to have things and death..

But the universe is not the one doing the giving.....

.....But that's another subject.

Note:" The name of a demon simply shows what tool he uses to gain entrance into the temple of your body." We all must be aware of Satan and his helpers. We must also know how they work.

This book is the first step,realizing you have an enemy,and knowing how he works.

(2 Corinthians ch.2 : 11)

We must not be ignorant of his devices. Every day we fight the good fight of faith by remembering the words of Yeshua,by thinking only good things,having a good attitude,and praying to the Lord Yeshua,talking to him as a friend and knowing that he hears us. Even if you get bad news you must realize that it could always be worse and that you are still blessed. Keep your confidence!!!!

Remember your enemy has a plan,he wants us all to be lost...... However you have the answer...

It's in your mouth....If you think and say the right things...the wrong things can't stop you.

Think about it,everything you interact with in this world you use your hands. To open a door you use your hand. To eat food,you use your hand. To gain access to what we need we use our hands....

But....in the spirit world things go a little different.

Well for starters you can't see spirits or spiritual things...you can't hold them...or move them.

Your hands are useless in the spirit realm......but what you do with your hands in the natural,

You do with your thoughts and words in the spirit!!

You work in the spirit by thinking and speaking.......(Matthew ch.16 : 19)We have the keys and when we pray we bind and loose things first by thinking it and then speaking it.......

You can truly receive the blessings of God, But you must be aware of your enemy.

(Philippians ch.4 : 8)

Finally Brethren,think only on the good things and the bad things will slowly go away. The reason why it is so important to think this way is because you create positive energy. Positive energy pushes negative energy away.

You must resist the devil and he will flee from you......Resist with your mind. With Positive Energy! When you here bad news start saying good news. Speak positive to a negative situation and watch the dry bones come together.

Pray in the name of Yeshua and the Demons will flee. You Have The Power.

This is one thing that your enemy does not want you to know. If you are a disciple of Christ,if he is your Lord and savior....you have been given the power over the enemy.

(Luke ch.9 : 1 - 2)

We have been given power over " ALL " devils and to cure diseases. We are to preach the Kingdom of God and heal the sick,give sight to the blind,fill the hungry,make the poor rich... and do all the things that Yeshua himself would do if he was here himself.....Because we are his body now. So,are you one of his disciples ?

You may say ," Yea but that was just for the first 12 disciples,not all of us!" Wrong again...read this

(Luke ch.10 : 1)

The Lord appointed,meaning he gave power of appointment to seventy other disciples also. Now if you continue to read in that same chapter you will come to verses 17 - 20.

(Luke ch.10 : 17 - 20)

Now all seventy of them are exited because the devils," demons," are subject to them though his name ,meaning that the demons obey the disciples.(Remember demons are fallen angels.) If only the disciples of today would speak to the demons today in the name of Yeshua and command them to go to the pit of hell.[19]Yeshua gives them power too....[20]The spirits,"demons,"are subject to them and the disciples names are written in heaven.

But even if all this does not fully convince you that you have this same power,maybe you need to see where ,"YOU" are in the scriptures. The real "secret"is found here>>>(Mark 9 : 38 - 40)

In this part of the scriptures we see that now it does not matter who you are,if you are for the Lord then you also can cast out devils and heal people as long as you obey and trust in the lord Yeshua. You see even though some people did not follow the Lord naturally,yet they followed him in the spirit,by obeying his teachings,which by the way were just extensions of what the Father already commanded>>Matt. 5 :18-19.

**************** (John ch.1 : 12) ******************

It does not matter how many people receive Yeshua as their Lord and obey him,To " THEM "he gives power to become a," Son of God ",just like him.....we are to be just like him. To have the spirit without measure,or limits,to do all the things he did and greater works than these. Once you know how to use the tools that God already gave you, then you can fix any thing. Remember,with God all things are possible. However some demons can only be driven out by Fasting and Prayer. This is why we must not waste time in the Lord. We have to grow in this way. Our measure of the spirit must grow within us. We should spend more time becoming a Son of God. This requires fasting,praying,meditating and study of the bible. The more you read and hear the word of the Lord the more faith you will have because faith comes by hearing...and hearing by the word of God is how we get more faith.>>>(Romans 10 : 17)

You Have The Power

(John ch.10 : 16)

In this scripture Christ refers to me and you..." If you have accepted him as your savior," then we are his sheep too,we are just not in the same fold as those sheep....Remember Mark 9 : 38 - 40,we had not been born yet. However there will be one fold one day and one shepherd. Not only this but our Lord even prayed for us. Now if anybody can get a prayer through, it is him.

>>>>>>>>>>>>>(John ch.14 : 12)<<<<<<<<<<<<

Yeshua is gone up in heaven now so if you believe in him,you can do the same works that he did and greater works than these! Because he has sent his Holy Spirit. The sign of power that let's you and everyone else know that you have this spirit, is when you and them can see the manifestation of the fruits of the spirit. You remember those right?Love,joy,peace,patience, meekness, gentleness, goodness, temperance, and faithfulness. This is in Galatians 5 : 27.

(John ch.17 : 15 - 22)

The powerful knowledge that is in this scripture that ties us to the rest of the disciples is verse 20.

The Lord Yeshua prays for ," Them ",also which shall believe on him though their word.

In case you missed it,If you believe in Yeshua the,"the anointed one," through the scriptures that the disciples left behind in the bible concerning him..this means you are one of his disciples too,You have been adopted in the family,and once you are in the family, you have the same benefits as all the rest of the disciples. The key word here is ," Adoption."

(Romans ch.8 : 15)

We have received the spirit of adoption from God and are Sons of God. We are little Christ's running around doing what the big Christ himself would do. Of course there are a few requirements to have this power,You must be a " Disciple of Yeshua."A follower of "him,"not Jesus. When we call the lord Jesus we are making reference to him,we are referring to him and there is nothing wrong with that,However the facts that I present in the beginning of this book still stand and in your personal relationship with the Lord,you must call on his name,"not refer to him."You must fast,pray and study to build up your faith. You must do what the Lord taught in the Gospels.

(John ch.8 : 31 - 32)

If we obey him and do what he says we are to do in the bible,we are his disciples,"indeed." Or in the deeds we do. This is how you know if you or anyone is his follower,by what you are doing. Are you doing the fruits of the Spirit?Is there a showing of them in your life?

Many Christians loose their power to rule over demons simply because They know not the true name of the Lord and they do not fully obey the word of God,you know,those" ten commandments."However when you are obedient to the Word of God ,you are given the right to rule over all devils.

This has been promised to you by Yeshua Himself.

He promised you that. We must all be aware of our enemy and how he works,so stay positive and think on good things and good things will happen. Stay confident in the Lord and fight for your faith,don't give up. Be content with what you have and if you need anything, pray to God and he will not let you down. Say the right things and the right things will come to pass.

Now that you have read this book be on the look out for my next book because it will truly be a blessing to all that read it.

This next book helps you understand what will soon come to the body of the Messiah.

Obtain as much knowledge as you can,and may the word of God dwell in you and keep you in perfect peace.

May Yeshua bless you.

J.T. Young

ABOUT THE AUTHOR.

JT Young is currently an ordained elder in the Church Of God In Christ and is an assistant to the pastor of Gospel Mission C.O.G.I.C., Sunday school superintendent,teacher of the men classes and also the drummer and sometimes the musician. He sometimes speak at speaking engagements at some churches and is known for being one who seeks the truth. He also works in the mining industry. This has not always been his life of course. There has been many ups and downs yet the Lord has delivered,trained,shaped and molded him into the man he is today.